Long Distance Relationship Guide

A Simple Guide for Christian with Tips on How to Make A Long Distance Relationship Work

T C Hill

Printed in the United States of America

ISBN: 1483985466
ISBN-13: 978-1483985466

DEDICATION

I want to dedicate this book to all who are struggling in their long-distance relationship. It is my hope that this book will help you well grounded and give you some insight in managing your long-distance relationship. All the best in your long distance relationship.

CONTENTS

PREFACE

The Guide for the Guide

By the end of this guide, you might think, "the title tricked me. It's not going to be easy to do this at all!" Let's clear all that up. We're talking about human relationships here. Boiling water is simple to understand AND easy to do, but relationships are different. This guide will be simple in that it intends to provide practical, understandable advice for those particular Christian (or curious non-Christian) couples who choose to (or are forced to) maintain a long-distance romantic relationship. However, maintaining a thriving romantic relationship of any sort is anything but easy or simple. It takes work. It asks that two people swallow a greater part of their selves in order to contribute to the well-being and functioning of the whole bond. But all this work is for something worth fighting for. Romance is the spice of life and true love, an aspect of life's great and ultimate purpose. That purpose is, of course, doing whatever it takes to meet up with God in His kingdom.

You might be searching particularly for some ideas on what you can do with your significant other while in a long-distance relationship. You will find those tidbits in the second half of the guide, but that information is secondary to the first half of the guide. The first half of this guide all about the habits of successful Christian couples. It's about attitudes and behaving in a way that promotes the longevity of the relationship, whether newly formed or bonded for years and years. While this guide specifies long-distance Christian relationships, it's rather important to recognize that overcoming distance really depends on how strong a relationship is to begin with. If a relationship is built on Christian values and that's what two people find to be of utmost importance, then it would follow that if the Christian aspect were to diminish, the relationship would ultimately come to an end, long-distance or not. Before we even address the "how to cope" techniques, it's irresponsible to simply assume every couple has a thriving and unshakable relationship. It's more realistic to assume that every relationship, no matter how unique, require a few key principles that are vital to it's health and that the long-distance aspect is just another obstacle to overcome over a bevy of other obstacles. I'm talking about components that every relationship should generally have.

Some might think that they can do without these principles or they may already possess the foundation; some people think they exempt from what generally occurs with everyone else. That may be true. However, even so, it never hurts to do a double-check one again, critically examine whatever you find important, and maybe perhaps, accept that there's always room for improvement.

That's the whole idea. At the end of the day, we're all human, capable of the greatest good and consequently, the greatest evil. Left alone, we have a bit of room to be selfish. However, with another person involved, the equation changes entirely. We're called to give more rather than take more. What's the best gift one person can give an-other? Why surely, it must be the best version of oneself – to put forth the best foot. It's not about putting up a polished façade - it's about genuinely trying to be a better person for the people you care about. We can all work to be a little bit better, regardless of why or for whom. This is the call of the Christian. Thankfully, we have God to aid us in that. Take the Scripture verses at the beginning of each section with you - the Word is the key to wisdom. Most importantly, begin and end all things with prayer. There will be many prayers from a multitude of sources scattered about - I encourage you to make use of them.

For the Non-Christian readers

This guide, while written specifically for the Christian audience, is still inclusive for any other audience that might read it. While much of the information presented here come from and are reasoned with the Christian perspective, the advice is nonetheless practical whether you subscribe to the Christian faith or not. I invite you to stick around, for there might be something useful for you.

God of my life,

I give you thanks and praise that I have life,
and that my life is filled with touches of your love.
You have given me a heart that wants to be happy,
and You have placed in me a desire to make a difference.
Quiet the fears and distractions of my heart long enough
for me to listen to the movement of Your Spirit to hear your
gentle invitation.
Reveal to me the choices that will make me happy.
Help me to discover my identity.
Let me understand how best to use the gifts
You have so lovingly lavished upon me
in preparation for our journey together.
And give me the courage to choose You as You have chosen
me.
Lord, let me know myself and let me know You.
In this is my happiness.

CHAPTER I: BEING THE BEST VERSION OF ONESELF

"Therefore, if anyone is in Christ, the new creation has come;
The old has gone, the new is here!"
2 Corinthians 5:17

"Do your best to present yourself to God as one approved, a worker who
does not need to be ashamed and who correctly handles the word of truth."
2 Timothy 2:15

"But to you who are listening I say: Love your enemies, do good to those
who hate you, bless those who curse you, pray for those who mistreat you. If
someone slaps you on one cheek, turn to them the other also. If someone takes
your coat, do not withhold your shirt from them. Give to everyone who asks
you, and if anyone takes what be-longs to you, do not demand it back.
Do to others as you would have them do to you."
Luke 6:27-31

"Love is patient, love is kind. It does not envy, it does not boast, it is not
proud. It does not dishonor others, it is not self-seeking, it is not easily
angered, it keeps no record of wrongs.
Love does not delight in evil but rejoices with the truth. It always protects,
always trusts, always hopes, always perseveres."
1 Corinthians 13:4-7

A few years ago, I was temporarily on location in Texas to develop and document new assistance programs for senior citizens in poverty. I was completely consumed with work. I

1

spent 12 hours each day conducting interviews, digging up research, and writing a dizzying amount of case notes. But despite being busy, I was distracted. I was in love with Celeste, a longtime high school friend that directly aided in my conversion to the Christian faith. I realized it a few months prior at a young adults conference when I saw her on stage giving a testimony. There she was, the great love that I had been searching for, right in my life this whole time.

You should know that I'm a very aggressive sort of person. When I resolve to go after something, courage from seemingly nowhere bubbles up and gets me running full speed towards whatever it is. Life takes a certain amount of boldness, but courage should be checked so it is not rash or impulsive. Thankfully, as I have grown in my life, my wisdom matured alongside it. Now, even as the drive courses through, my mind halts everything in order to think things through.

When I first realized my affection for her at the conference, I took pause. This wasn't the first time I had ever been struck with the idea that I could be looking at my future spouse. From what I knew of the general science of attraction, there are chemicals at play that may skew my logical reasoning. I knew that if I wanted to assess the legitimacy of what I was seeing and feeling, I have to let the test of time level things out. I had to pray about it; consult trusted confidants, friends, and pastors; and look for indication of where God might be directing me at that moment in my life.

It took five months of prayer-heavy discernment to reach the decision to pursue Celeste. I had to tread carefully: not only would I be initiating what may be a permanent change in our friendship, courting her and being with her would be difficult because she lived across the country. If I was going to pursue her, I couldn't do it in person just yet. Even if we began a relationship, eventually we would find ourselves separated again. A long-distance relationship was inevitable at some point. I took a hard look at myself. If I really loved her, it would demand all of me to love her. Not only that, if I in-tend on being the person she goes "all in" for, I had to be someone worthy of her. This was a big moment for me. I have had a lot of opportunities to be with girls who might have been my great love, but at the very last moment, I was not convinced. Not this time. I saw this woman as the best person for me. But this beautiful fact came with another realization of my own self: if I demanded the best for myself, then she has that same right to demand the best for herself. Therefore, am I the best I can be? Am I the best version of myself?

Before we dive into anything, whether you're in a relationship or not, ask yourself these questions: **Am I the best version of myself? If not, am I on my way there? Am I a gift to the person I love? What do I have to offer as a person in this relationship?**

Maybe you are – that's wonderful. I certainly wasn't. At the very least, I'm trying my best. I'm willing to bet that most of us aren't even close to the best version of our-selves. Some might counter this notion and remark, "if it is true love, then shouldn't a person just accept another person for who he/she is?" That is true, but only to an extent. Accepting someone is about forgiving them for their wrongdoings and what shortcomings they might have - it is a very loving thing to do. But being the best version of your-self is a personal responsibility. It depends on how much you really value the per-son you're with. In fact, it really depends on how much you value any person you come into contact with. When I prepare Celeste my famous cream-cheese stuffed French toast, I want it to be the very best it can taste. When I look for a place where my grand-mother should get her healthcare, I look for the best possible place. Likewise, if I can improve myself in a way that better serves my friends, family, and especially the person I'm madly in love with, then I don't see why shouldn't.

We're never going to reach perfection - at least not until we're united with God Himself. However, we can come to love and forgive the shortcomings of other people. That's love. In the meantime, we can also work on ourselves to try to reduce our own shortcomings - it's about making the self into a gift that blesses others. That's love, too. That means letting go of simply thinking about what I want or need and thinking of others. It means that when I get angry or frustrated that I endure and be patient. It means that if I'm vulnerable to a particular sin or habit, that I work diligently with God to over-come it. The person I love deserves the most I can offer. It never hurts to consistently pause in life, take a breath, and ask this question in prayer. Being the best version of yourself is more than just something incredibly beneficial for the self and for those around the person, it's what we're called to do as Christians.

So ask yourself, "Am I the best version of my self?"

The Prayer of St. Francis

Lord, make me an instrument of your peace.
Where there is hatred, let me sow love;
Where there is injury, pardon;
Where there is doubt, faith;
Where there is despair, hope;
Where there is darkness, light;
Where there is sadness, joy.
O Divine Master, grant that I may not so much seek
To be consoled as to console;
To be understood as to understand;
To be loved as to love.
For it is in giving that we receive;
It is in pardoning that we are pardoned;
And it is in dying that we are born to eternal life.

CHAPTER II: THE LONG-DISTANCE RELATIONSHIP

… May the Lord keep watch between you and me when we are away from each other.
Genesis 31:49

> *Upon my bed at night*
> *I sought him whom my soul loves;*
> *I sought him, but found him not;*
> *I called him, but he gave no answer.*
>
> *I will rise now and go about the city,*
> *in the streets and in the squares;*
> *I will seek him whom my soul loves."*
> *I sought him, but found him not.*
> *The sentinels found me,*
> *as they went about in the city.*
> *"Have you seen him whom my soul loves?"*
>
> *Scarcely had I passed them,*
> *when I found him whom my soul loves.*
> *I held him, and would not let him go*
> *until I brought him into my mother's house,*
> *and into the chamber of her that conceived me.*
Song of Solomon 3:1-4

So it's come to this: you or your significant other are given an opportunity or forced into a situation where one or the other must live in another state or country. Going away to school, a job opportunity, volunteer work over borders or overseas; it could be for any reason. When Celeste and I started dating, we were fortunate enough to spend the first few months together at home in Nevada. However, the joy would be short-lived; she was due to transfer to a university in Illinois. We knew it was coming, but it was difficult to swallow. We would be separated by a distance of 1,700 miles, a bit of a change from our 20-minute drive from anywhere to anywhere at home. How will this distance impact our relationship? What does this all really mean?

The long-distance relationship merely introduces an increase in distance between two people, thereby decreasing convenience. Convenience is a big factor here. Obviously, the further the distance, the more difficult and costly it would be to take time to visit the other person. For many people, this is an unaffordable luxury. This, in turn, de-creases the amount of time one has to physically spend with another person. In a romantic relationship, physical and proximal intimacy contributes a great deal to the establishing and strengthening of the emotional bond formed between two people.

What does this mean over time? As the opportunity for proximal connection with one another decreases, the demand for other means of connection increase. Conversation begins to weigh more heavily. For many, a deep sense of longing borne from the void of physical touch manifests itself as a deeper emotional need. Of all the clichés one could conjure up to soothe a pair of lovers separated by miles, "distance makes the heart grow fonder" does certainly hold a kernel of truth. Of course, as with most oversimplified things, it's not mentioned that more often than not, the fondness can mutate into intense feelings of loneliness, jealousy, depression, and unfortunately in some cases, in-fidelity.

Thankfully, most long-distance relationships are temporary, lasting maybe a few months to only a few years or so. However, for those couples who might be separated indefinitely, it is an entirely different and tragic matter – one might even question if the relationship should continue. That's another matter we won't mention here - every relationship is different. Fortunately, for those couples separated by distance within a limited timeframe, it's only a matter of outlasting the duration of separation by finding other ways to connect or cope. Patience is obviously going to be very important. Additionally, if the relationship was already thriving prior to the distance, dealing with the distance merely means finding new activities to maintain and strengthen the bonds in lieu of what is no longer convenient. Even more so, while physical and proximal attachment is important, there are certainly more methods to grow together as a couple.

It's silly to assume that every couple reading this guide is perfect. Realistically, couples fight, undergo difficult times, and feel the sting of the world's demands in con-junction with maintaining a mature relationship. That's what the movies don't tell any-one about being in relationship. There are a lot of benefits in being with another person, but it's not all sunshine and daisies. In general, romantic relationships take a great deal of work to maintain. It involves accepting and loving even the things that you may not like about another person. Being with someone means taking them as the whole person, not just the shiny, polished parts. Nowadays, it seems almost more likely for a couple to break up than to remain together indefinitely. Long-distance relationships add an even greater strain to that. Contact methods narrow down to phone calls and e-mail; meeting up for dates or going on trips becomes a costly chore that requires greater time and financial investments; and if one person becomes too busy or if communication is un-clear, the sense of interrelatedness could diminish. The relationship becomes a job and a half, demanding more patience while receiving less of the instantly gratifying proximal benefits.

But, alas, love prevails. Typically, people are willing to go the extra miles, literally and figuratively, for one another. While their success is a different story, people are nonetheless eager to go to bat for their significant other. I have many married and engaged friends who courted their spouses and fiancés exclusively over a distance of several states that have relationships more wildly successful than couples I've known who are living within the same city. How did they do it? In addition to outlasting the time apart, it's about making the most out of a situation. The key is to take the supposed disadvantages presented by the distance problem and turning them into productive advantages.

Irish Blessing
May the road rise to meet you,
May the wind be always at your back,
May the sun shine warm upon your face,
The rains fall soft upon your fields and
Until we meet again,
May God hold you in the palm of His hand.

What are the advantages of being in a LDR?

O Lord, all my longing is known to you; my sighing is not hidden from
you.
Psalm 38:9

Do not fear, for I am with you,
Do not be afraid, for I am your God;
I will strengthen you, I will help you,
I will uphold you with my victorious right hand.
Isaiah 49:10

The first most apparent advantage is the fondness borne from longing and loneliness one might expect the distance can induce. Initially, the distance might actually work wonders to strengthen attachment, as a new change alters the general dynamic of the relationship. This could lead to a greater appreciation of proximal connection later on. However, if left unchecked and untamed, this fondness might mutate into dependence or obsession, thereby hindering a person's everyday life.

The second benefit is extra time to oneself. This surplus of time can be used to achieve personal goals and focus on individual growth. While personal growth should be the emphasized always regardless of distance, being physically apart puts an individual in a position where it's demanded, especially since any dependence will become readily apparent once the separation occurs. It's important to realize that there needs to be a balance between being how much you depend on your partner and how much you depend on yourself. There is no simple solution here. Too much independence can leave a couple feeling disconnected and unrelated, whereas too much dependence puts a strain on the individual. A couple is, after all, the sum of two individuals. Typically, people are attracted to one another's individuality, despite the oneness that accrues eventually. In addition to personal growth, one has more freedom to pursue personal interests.

The third advantage is the opportunity to reconnect with other relationships in your life (i.e. friends, families, community, church, etc) that may have been neglected or put off to the side. Exclusive romantic relationships are very time consuming and typically, while it's understandable, people get left behind. The added benefit here is that maintaining healthy relationships with other people can also help you "practice" for your romantic relationship with your partner.

The fourth advantage is the opportunity for the couple to get to know each other on a deeper intellectual, emotional, and spiritual level. With the physical and proximal connection out of the picture, a couple is forced to find other means of connection. You'll be surprised - there's always something you can learn about the person you love. The world is rich with experience and being able to live each day blesses us with the gift of gaining new knowledge, especially from the person you love.

The fifth benefit is particular to Christians, as the temptation to lust and the championing of purity and chastity are evident. Long-distance relationships reduce physical and proximal connection, thereby reducing tempting factors. It's no mystery that people who fall into lust often get carried away with something that starts off seemingly innocent. Distance adds to direct removal of immediate tempting situations. It should noted, of course, that a couple should be guarded when reunited after a period of time - the attachment born from longing can excite passions that must be kept in check.

The Serenity Prayer

God, grant me the serenity to accept the things I cannot change,
The courage to change the things I can, and the wisdom to know the
difference.
Living one day at a time, enjoying one moment at a time,
Accepting hardships as the pathway to peace,
Taking, as Jesus did,
This sinful world as it is, not as I would have it,
Trusting that you will make all things right.
If I surrender to your will,
So that I may be reasonably happy in this life,
And supremely happy with You, forever in the next.
Amen.

CHAPTER III: A COUPLE FOCUSED ON CHRIST

Jesus replied: "Love the Lord your God with all your heart and with all your soul and with all your mind." This is the first and greatest commandment. And the second is like it: "Love your neighbor as yourself."
Matthew 22:37-39

You were taught, with regard to your former way of life, to put off your old self, which is being corrupted by its deceitful desires; to be made new in the attitude of your minds; and to put on the new self, created to be like God in true righteousness and holiness. Therefore each of you must put off falsehood and speak truthfully to your neighbor, for we are all members of one body.
Ephesians 4:22-25

I know full well what kind of woman Celeste is: she is a God-fearing woman who chooses to live her life modestly, honestly, and faithfully. She is utterly devoted and in love with God before all things and every bit of her exuded such devotion. As a man, I knew that in order to win her heart, I would have to prove worthy. When we started the relationship, the greatest priority we set was to stay fixated on Christ as a couple.

When asked about the greatest law, Jesus essentially spelled out the most concise yet profound summary of the Christian life: to love God with all one's heart, soul, and mind and to love one's neighbor as much as he loves himself. Jesus referred to these two rules as the Great Commandments.

A Christian is as Christian as he chooses to be. It's more

than just believing in God and going to church. It's about following through with what Christ is teaching us, that is, to live a life focused on God and therefore, focused on loving your neighbor. This means realizing the potential of oneself in order to be a gift and blessing for the sake of others. This also means to do no hurt to any person and furthermore, forgiving anyone who hurts you. It's a tall order because it calls us to give more than we can spare at any time, regardless of how we feel, to everyone. This may seem obvious to some, but being a Christian means following the example Jesus set with his life.

Therefore be imitators of God, as beloved children, and live in love, as Christ loved us and gave himself up for us, a fragrant offering and sacrifice to God.
Ephesians 5:1-2

This guide is written for couples currently in or on the verge of entering into a long-distance relationship. Now, how "Christian" a couple is depends entirely on the couple. What I mean by that is that being a Christian couple is more than just two Christians coming together romantically. Typically, a romantic Christian relationship implies at the very least a discerned, chaste, and giving relationship reliant and centered on Jesus. These characteristics are considered typical because they distinguish the key difference between a Christian couple and any other else. Without these characteristics, a couple is just like any other couple. As mentioned before, being a Christian is more than just claiming a system of belief – it's following through with those beliefs. A Christian relationship, therefore, depends on how much a couple prioritizes Jesus, His teachings, and how they ought to practice their Christian faith.

A couple actively trying to keep Christ in their relationship could easily make a long-distance commitment an opportunity for growth. Physical and proximal attachment can often birth lustful temptation; therefore, being apart can help a couple remain chaste and focus on getting to know each other more on a emotional, intellectual, and spiritual level. With the existence of phone and video chatting, being apart does nothing to stop a couple from praying together Bible study can be conducted over a variety of communication mediums and furthermore, a test of distance can really prove to be a worthy

12

test of one's patience, commitment, and fidelity. Even more so, separation frees up time for the individuals to dedicate to service within their own community and church.

St. Augustine's Prayer to the Holy Spirit

Breathe in me, O Holy Spirit, that my thoughts may all be holy.
Act in me, O Holy Spirit, that my work, too, may be holy.
Draw my heart, O Holy Spirit, that I love but what is holy.
Strengthen me, O Holy Spirit, to defend all that is holy.
Guard me, then, O Holy Spirit, that I always may be holy.
Amen.

CHAPTER IV: ON DATING WITH PURPOSE

Looking Ahead Towards Marriage

Then the Lord God said, "It is not good that the man should be alone;
I will make him a helper as his partner.

So the Lord God caused a deep sleep to fall upon the man, and he slept;
then he took one of his ribs and closed up its place with flesh. And the rib
that the Lord God had taken from the man he made into a woman and
brought her to the man. Then the man said,

"This at last is bone of my bones and flesh of my flesh;
this one shall be called Woman, for out of Man this one was taken."

Therefore a man leaves his father and his mother and clings to his wife,
and they become one flesh.

Genesis 2:18; 2:21-24

Why are you two together?

Many times, people let their emotions take them for a ride and jump into a relationship without even asking this question. Sometimes, two people discover that their "gamble" to invest in a person pays off and they end up marrying that person. However, most people aren't that fortunate. Rather, once the initial attraction and rush of romance fades away, two people finally realize the real nature of one another. Attraction, by it's very purpose, is meant to be distracting. However, the true love and "work" of a relationship surfaces after these feelings fade away.

For the intention to marry some may gasp, "It's far too soon!" It is important to consider what the point of a romantic relationship is really about. While it's typical for couples to put off even discussing the prospect of marriage until they know each other really well, that poses a problem. Suppose a couple is together for several years but ultimately decides that they're not meant to be married. What would all that time and ef-fort been for? Assuming these individuals were completely devoted to one another, they would have been giving to one another for no particular reason. With two people together, are they together with an intention to one day marry...or break up? Why pursue a relationship at all? To satisfy loneliness?

While it might take a bit of confidence for someone to simply announce that they're going to marry someone right upon entering the relationship, it's more about de-fining the purpose of the relationship. This places tremendous weight on the prayer and discernment involved in figuring out whether or not a relationship is for you. It's about where two people are going and how they're going to get there. It's also quite important because it puts a heavy stake on the overall relationship. If two people have discerned that they are going to get married, the long-distance relationship seems merely like an obstacle to overcome rather than a potential deal breaker. Overall, it's about making the most use out of time with one another.

Celeste was different from any woman I had ever come to love. We were friends to begin with - I knew her thoroughly before I even fell in love with her. The good, the bad, the ugly, and most importantly, the kind of person she was and the person she was becoming, it was as clear as day and unclouded by the raptures of attraction that blur reality. In the past, I would develop feelings for someone almost instantaneously and rush to start a romance with that person while hoping to get to know her along the way. However, once I got to know them well enough, I discovered that I didn't want to pursue anything like that with them. I wanted to get married and I wanted the efforts to go completely towards my future spouse. This made sense. A dating relationship is, after all, an exclusive, romantic friendship with some degree of commitment. But even as well as I knew her, I wanted to take a great deal of time really figuring out if pursuing her was what I wanted to do.

But why get married at all? Divorce is staggeringly prevalent in the United States - many people wonder what the purpose of marriage actually serves. Why can't two people just be together and if they remain together forever, let that be it? From Scripture, we learn of God's call for us to marry one another in faith and love. He calls us to belong to one another and become one, indivisible unit committed to the preservation of family and community. In the third chapter of Matthew, Jesus is questioned by the Pharisees on divorce, citing Moses' early allowance for couples to separate. Jesus replies eloquently, "...a man shall leave his father and mother and be joined to his wife, and the two shall become one flesh'? So they are no longer two, but one flesh. Therefore what God has joined together, let no one separate." He goes on to say, "It was because you were so hard-hearted that Moses allowed you to divorce your wives, but from the beginning it was not so."

The gift of marriage is the celebration of the unbreakable union between a man and a woman. To put it simply, marriage is the promise of two willing individuals saying to one another, "I won't quit on you. I'll give it all for you." It must be a mutual exchange of love, commitment, and effort. By very nature and definition, marriage and subsequently, family life, is the summit of human relationship. Getting married and raising a family embodies every Christian value there is: unconditional gratitude, generosity, diligence, and most importantly, sacrifice. Therefore, how much are you willing to give to the one you love? Do you love someone enough to pledge to be with that person forever and more importantly, follow through with your promise? If a person isn't ready to face even this question, then I daresay they're not ready for a mature, purpose-driven relationship. The relationship is just a step towards the ultimate goal, marriage and family.

Prayer for God's Will

My God, My God
My human words of deep adoration and gratitude could never adequately
express how wonderful You are to me. You have weaved every moment of my
life into existence. You love me dearly and choose to involve Yourself in the
details of my life, even though I am so small.
Help me to discern, Father, the great purposes of my life and the plans
You have for me. Give me the courage to face the unknown and the faith in
knowing You are with me and for me. Whatever You are calling me to do,
my Love, I am eager because I love You.
Amen

CHAPTER V: ON PRAYER

*Ask, and it will be given you; search, and you will find; knock, and the
door will be opened for you. For everyone who asks receives, and everyone who
searches finds, and for everyone who knocks, the door will be opened.*
Matthew 7:7-8

*You may as soon find a living man that does not breath,
as a living Christian that does not pray.*
Matthew Henry (1662-1714)

Sometimes, I hear some people moan, "I pray to God
all day for (this) or (that), but He doesn't come through!" Other
times, I run into people who have stopped praying altogether. A
former atheist friend of mine used to ask me, "Why pray? If God
is all-knowing, why do you even have to say anything at all? Can't
he just read your mind?" The answer is incredibly relevant to this
guide: prayer is about communication and cultivating a
relationship with God.

Drawing from the first half of the Great
Commandment, to "love the Lord your God with all your heart
and with all your soul and with all your mind", prayer is about the
decision of a person to maintain that relationship with God
Himself. It's an act of faith and more so, it's an act of love. God
is incredibly personal and even more essential, living. God isn't a
machine who spews out blessings to those who pray versus
punishments for those who don't. Rather, God likes to get up

close and personal and involved in the lives of the creation He loves so dearly. Jesus is the greatest example, of course. He came as a friend, a brother, and servant despite being cut from a higher cloth. Not only did He constantly talk to God, but most of His ministry involved building relation-ships with his followers! It's about communication and sharing in each other's lives. In fact, understanding prayer as communication and how that communication is necessary for a vibrant and life-giving relationship with God comments a great deal on what ingredients might be essential for human relationships as well.

In reality, almost anything can be categorized as a prayer. An Our Father, a charismatic praise and worship session, a makeshift word jumble of praise, a breath of gratitude, even a silent act of kindness to a stranger – as far as this faith is concerned, prayer is normally considered the easiest thing to do. You quiet down, tune in, and speak. However, it's not uncommon for people to let prayer become dried up and routine (or forget to pray altogether). The reason is this: it's not difficult to pray, but rather, it is difficult to pray consistently, day by day. This takes more than just the urge to pray – this also means praying when you don't have enough time, or when you don't feel up to it, or even when you have nothing to say. Make time. Make words. Communicate. God wants to know you by you wanting to know Him. He knows what you're going to say, but what's important is that friendship that takes two to build together.

Friendship is the key. Romance and intimacy aside, the friendship is the core of almost every sort of meaningful relationship. Without it, once the romance and intimacy fades away, two people are left with very little to stick around for. Just like a person's friendship with God, communication is absolutely vital for the cultivation of the human relationship. Therefore, when you think of prayer, think of it as communication, which is the means for building a friendship with a God already arrived halfway with His in-tense love. Learn how to build a friendship with God and relationships with everyone else, especially your partner, become more vibrant as well.

Our Father, Who is in heaven,
Holy is Your Name;
Your kingdom come,
Your will be done,
on earth as it is in heaven.
Give us this day our daily bread,
and forgive us our sins,
as we forgive those who sin against us;
and lead us not into temptation,
but deliver us from evil. Amen.

On Praying Alone

But whenever you pray, go into your room and shut the door and pray to your Father who is in secret; and your Father who sees in secret will reward you.
Matthew 6:6

Rejoice always, pray without ceasing, give thanks in all circumstances; for this is the will of God in Christ Jesus for you.
1 Thessalonians 5:16-18

Before we dive into the next section, "On Praying Together", I want to address the importance of praying alone. As mentioned before, our God is absolutely personal. He wants to know you. He wants to know me. But our faith journey, while shared with the community in many ways, is also a unique, intimate, and individual experience. God may speak to you in ways that may not speak as loudly to me. However, God may also speak to me in ways that may not jump out for you. Imagine a car manufacturer that sells cars with custom car seat perfectly tailored for each customer's bottom and back. In a way, God is like that manufacturer, but rather than car seats for backs and bottoms, He tailors the words He needs to say to each and every one of us completely dependent on how different we all are.

Therefore, if you're not used to praying often by yourself, now's the best time to start. Even when you're praying often with the person you're with, don't let that be the only time you find yourself communicating with God. Find time to pray by yourself, as well. Loving God with all your heart, mind, and soul takes precedent over any other relationship you'll ever have. This is absolutely vital. Keep Christ in your own personal life - there's no one of greater importance. Not only will this keep you rooted in Christ, but it'll give you the means to cope with loneliness and adversity that may be encountered later on. Additionally, you'll also have a very rich, personal spiritual life to contribute to your own relationship.

My dear Jesus,
I am in awe when I realize how small I am compared to how great You are. Yet, You still listen to my prayers and bless my life as if I was the only one You see. Be with me, Oh Lord, through my brightest and darkest moments. I want to share my life with You, as You as so willing given up Your life for me.
Even as I sit here quietly worshipping You, the opportunity to do so alone is a gift.
May my prayers echo the gratitude that I feel being Your loved child.
Amen

On Praying Together

Again, truly I tell you that if two of you on earth agree about anything they ask for, it will be done for them by my Father in heaven. For where two or three gather in my name, there am I with them.
Matthew 18:19-20

Let's connect this with the couple-relationship. Bringing together the concepts from the previous two sections, if prayer is basically communication with God, then it would behoove the Christian couple to pray together. As two individuals pursuing a deep friendship with God, why not combine forces and make it a group activity? Matthew 18:19-20 spells that very idea out. Now, as mentioned several times, the Great Commandments are central to what makes a Christian relationship "Christian". Even in an exclusive romantic relationship, we still continue to remain in fellowship with the Lord fervently and consistently. However, one of the most wonderful things in being in an exclusive relationship with another Christian is how much you can share with the other person. Pray together, study Scripture together, serve together, share Christ with the world together - you're teammates playing for a divine franchise.

Furthermore, whether you're together or alone, it should be a habit to pray for other people. Consider this: measuring a person by the minutes of their life, to spend time lifting up the needs of others to God is utterly selfless. Not only is it a great act of faith, but it is an act of love for those who are prayed for. Believe it or not, you probably have people praying for you every day without you even knowing it! Be a prayer warrior for others.

My dear Jesus,
By Your will, You have given us the body of Christ - our brothers and sisters - as a community for each other on this earth. In them we see You, Lord, and in each other, we fulfill Your call to love beyond ourselves and beyond what we think is possible. As we gather to pray together, we are united with the prayers of our brothers and sisters everywhere, lifting up our minds to heaven. Lord, bless us as we strive in our lives to grow in the Spirit and live to love You and one another. Holy Spirit, burn within us and enable us to be like Christ as He loved.
Amen

On Discernment

And this is my prayer: that your love may abound more and more in knowledge and depth of insight, so that you may be able to discern what is best and may be pure and blameless for the day of Christ, filled with the fruit of righteousness that comes through Jesus Christ—to the glory and praise of God.
Philippians 1:9-11

Pray for us; we are sure that we have a clear conscience, desiring to act honorably in all things.
Hebrews 13:18

Earlier, I mentioned how I spent a great deal of time discerning before I was able to conclude that my pursuit of Celeste was appropriate for that moment in my life. Discernment, defined in the Christian sense, is all about approaching the decision-making process with God. It's like asking for the insight of a trusted, more experienced friend, sibling, or mentor - but instead you're consulting God. Then, it's just a matter of communicating with Him by praying; looking to Scripture; consulting close family, friends, credible pastoral sources; objectively weighing pros and cons; and finally, exercising the virtue of prudence and adding a bit of courage. Discernment functions to help a person make the appropriate choice in any particular situation. Naturally, any two adults ought to really give a romantic relationship a real run through the obstacle of rational reasoning before commencement since a relationship is pretty serious business. There are plenty of things to consider:

1.   Where is this relationship going to go?
2.   How will our personalities, habits, behaviors, and values compliment/conflict?
3.   What are our short-term and long-term goals?
4.   What am I willing to invest in a relationship in terms of commitment?

These things seem like common sense questions to ask but as it generally turns out, when two people are attracted to each other and the gears of romance are moving, common sense doesn't remain all that common. With Celeste, I had to ask really practical questions that addressed whether or not I would be able to provide for her even de-spite the distance.

Now, as mentioned earlier, Christian discernment is more than this logical reasoning that any couple should visit – it's about how God factors into it all together with that critical analysis. In a way, discernment is about making the choice God would want a person to choose. When faced with the opportunity to give the homeless man you pass by the half-sandwich you plan on eating later, Christian discernment will draw upon Jesus' compassion for the poor. Assuming you're not going to die of starvation by giving up the half-sandwich, it would be imitative of Christ to dispense a little charity and compassion for someone in need. Likewise, discerning a relationship involves the use of your rational faculties and furthermore, how the teachings of Christ and where you are in your faith life impact that decision-making process.

Consider these questions:

1. How is my relationship with God? How is my partner's relationship with God?

2. How is my prayer life? How is my partner's prayer life?

3. Am I in a position in my life where I am continuously growing to be a better per-son?

4. In what ways am I leading my partner towards Christ?

5. Am I in this relationship just to satisfy personal loneliness?

6. Is this relationship making me a better Christian?

7. What is my capacity for patience?

8. What is my capacity for forgiveness?

9. What does unconditional love really mean?

10. Can I marry this person?

11. In all things, what is God calling me to do in this particular situation?

Obviously, these questions are quite intense and require a great deal of reflection and discussion. However, consider this: most of these questions revolve around Jesus and the Christian life. Others involve considering the other person. A relationship is a two-person endeavor and therefore, prioritizes selflessness. This draws directly from the Great Commandments, to "to love God with whole heart, mind, and soul and to love your neighbor as yourself ."

Getting back to what we were talking about, the concept of discernment basically calls for an individual to critically think and earnestly seek God for direction. As one can imagine, it's pretty important in every aspect of life. This is equally true for an exclusive couple relationship. Couples deal with problems and situations that they must face together. Discernment helps a couple to calmly solve problems while keeping Christ in the picture.

Old Sarum Prayer

God be in head and in my understanding;
God be in my eyes and in my looking;
God be in my mouth and in my speaking;
God be in my heart and in my thinking;
God be at my end and at my departing.
Amen

CHAPTER VI: HOW TO DEAL WITH OPPOSITION

The simple believe everything, but the clever consider their steps.
Proverbs 14:15

Where there is no guidance, a nation falls, but in an abundance of counselors there is safety.
Proverbs 11:14

Some of you may have already brooded over the pros and cons of the long-distance relationship with your partner, family, friends, and/or pastors and maybe per-haps, you may have found direct opposition to it. So what now? On one hand, the people you trust and consult are saying that the long-distance relationship isn't a good idea. On the other, depending on whether you have a choice or not and if the two of you don't intend to end the relationship, the long-distance aspect might be an advantageous opportunity for you and your partner.

There really is no cover-all answer here. Every situation differs from one another and vary in an infinite number of ways. However, there is a way to go about making the decision to pursue a long-distance relationship or not with the advice of your pastors and peers.

First, it's important to recognize that your family, friends, and pastors know you in a way that you seldom witness - the manifested self. An individual knows himself and the motivations (or lack of) behind each behavior, but outside perspectives reveal other insights. Think about the characteristics you know about your closest friends that they might not even realize they have - it's a side of themselves that they don't get the pleasure of witnessing like everyone else does. The point is that we come to know ourselves better by the help of the people around us. It's not a question of whether I know myself better or whether my friends know me better than I know myself - it's about putting together all perspectives to form one whole picture. That's one of the many benefits of being in community - others help us to realize our true selves.

With that, it's important to recognize that your friends and pastors probably love you and are thinking towards you and your partner's benefit. I say "probably" because I sincerely hope you don't have friends and pastors whom you trust who would do the contrary - unfortunately, that's not always the case.

You must consider the fact that your pastors/peers are looking out for you (how-ever accurate their assessment may be); what you and your partner determine what is viable to do as a couple; and what you feel God is calling you to do. Consider carefully. It's a sign of respect to adhere to someone else's advice (assuming it's sound and just) because it shows that one values their opinion. However, if you and your partner have discerned together and are realistic and reasonable in concluding that it's a good idea - talk it over with your family, friends, and pastors again. Whatever the conclusion is, en-sure that you're on good terms with everyone - being a couple is also about the people surrounding the relationship. Don't burn the bridges of your support systems if you out-right disagree - just because a long-distance relationship is doable doesn't necessarily mean it's the right decision.

My dearest Lord Jesus,
Oh, how I love You, my Lord! The great gift of life and the opportunity
to share our lives with so many other lives is a blessing beyond our
comprehension! I thank You for all the blessings of life, particularly the gift of
wisdom manifested through the Spirit of my friends, my family, my pastors,
and those who have walked this earth before us and set an amazing example
of holy living.
Create in me, Oh Lord, a heart of love and a mind of wisdom to properly
discern what I am to do in facing difficult decisions in my life.
In all things, Lord, constantly remind us to draw our eyes up to You in
all things, as You are the ultimate guide and hope of the universe.
I trust You, Lord. I love You, Lord.
Amen

CHAPTER VII: ON REMAINING CHASTE

"You shall not commit adultery."
Exodus 20:14

"But I say to you that everyone who looks at a woman with lust has already commit-ted adultery with her in his heart."
Matthew 5:28

"Blessed are the pure in heart, for they will see God."
Matthew 5:8

"Let no one despise your youth, but set the believers an example in speech and conduct, in love, in faith, in purity."
1 Timothy 4:12

"Now the works of the flesh are obvious: fornication, impurity, licentiousness, idolatry, sorcery, enmities, strife, jealousy, anger, quarrels, dissensions, factions, envy, drunkenness, carousing, and things like these. I am warning you, as I warned you before: those who do such things will not inherit the kingdom of God."
Galatians 5:19-20

"Flee from sexual immorality. Every other sin a person commits is outside the body, but the sexually immoral person sins against his own body. Or do you not know that your body is a temple of the Holy Spirit within you, whom you have from God? You are not your own, for you were bought with a price. So glorify God in your body."
1 Corinthians 6:18-20

"For God did not call us to impurity but in holiness"
1 Thessalonians 4:7

We're all human. We're easily tempted and naturally drawn to the allure of the flesh. Of the many things that Christian couples struggle with, the temptation of lust is perhaps the most often discussed and the most prevalent. Two people who are attracted to each other physically, emotionally, and spiritually and put in the same 5 meters - it's almost like we're set up to fail! Sex is a beautiful thing, but only when it's appropriate. For unmarried couples, Christ calls us to exercise self-control and pursue purity and holiness. Many of you reading this are probably already aware of the gravity lust can have in a particular situation. What does one do in that situation? The Bible literally tells us to get out of there! Flee! Depart! Remove the self from the situation. Chastity, like many of the virtues Christ calls us to, demands self-control.

With that in mind, a long-distance relationship might even seem like an ideal situation for two people to get to know each other on a much deeper level while at the same time, making it physically improbable to fall victim to lustful tendencies.

While the distance may be a very distinct advantage in remaining chaste, a couple should always be on guard. When Celeste and I would visit one another, the temptation of lust was even greater because of the deeper emotional attachment we had accrued being apart.

Psalm 51:1-17

Have mercy on me, O God,
according to your steadfast love; according to your abundant mercy
blot out my transgressions.
Wash me thoroughly from my iniquity, and cleanse me from my sin!
For I know my transgressions, and my sin is ever before me.
Against you, you only, have I sinned and done what is evil in your sight,
so that you may be justified in your words and blameless in your judgment.
Behold, I was brought forth in iniquity, and in sin did my mother conceive
me.

30

Behold, you delight in truth in the inward being, and you teach me wisdom in the secret heart.

Purge me with hyssop, and I shall be clean; wash me, and I shall be whiter than snow.

Let me hear joy and gladness; let the bones that you have broken rejoice.

Hide your face from my sins, and blot out all my iniquities.

Create in me a clean heart, O God, and renew a right spirit within me.

Cast me not away from your presence, and take not your Holy Spirit from me.

Restore to me the joy of your salvation, and uphold me with a willing spirit.

Then I will teach transgressors your ways, and sinners will return to you.

Deliver me from blood guiltiness, O God, O God of my salvation, and my tongue will sing aloud of your righteousness.

O Lord, open my lips,

and my mouth will declare your praise.

For you will not delight in sacrifice, or I would give it;

you will not be pleased with a burnt offering.

The sacrifices of God are a broken spirit;

a broken and contrite heart, O God, you will not despise.

Amen

CHAPTER VIII: HEALTHY HABITS OF THE SUCCESSFUL COUPLE

For surely I know the plans I have for you, says the Lord,
plans for your welfare and not for harm, to give you a future with hope.
Jeremiah 29:11

Let's not forget the facts here - the long-distance aspect might be difficult, but it isn't the hardest part. At the very core of the couple is the relationship dynamic. If two people were having a really rough time maintaining the relationship while together, the strain of distance won't make it any easier. While the means of maintaining the relation-ship change, the vital ingredients for successful and healthy relationships remain the same. As mentioned before, being in a relationship is about thinking and giving to one another, even if that means giving up something to achieve it. Most of this section will run into each other and revisit some of the information we've seen before. For that reason, I'd like to run through the principles rather quickly.

Communication

You must understand this, my beloved: let everyone be quick to listen,
slow to speak, slow to anger;
James 1:19

When I was a child, I spoke like a child, I thought like a child, I
reasoned like a child; when I became an adult, I put an end to childish ways.
1 Corinthians 13:11

The majority of your relationship will be how you and your partner communicate with one another. Getting to know each other, figuring out each other's preferences, working through conflict, and planning the future - there's no way around it. Discuss things openly, honestly, and with love. Listen actively, try to understand, and empathize with one another.

This is especially important when the two of you are in disagreement. I have known plenty of couples who fight nearly every day. People say it's an unfavorable form of communication. They're right, but also wrong. Most of the time, people fight because of the lack of communication in a situation. One person isn't willing to give up being right over the other, or perhaps they actually intend on saying something that would break down the other person. Being in a relationship means you have to think about the other person. That means there's compromise in order to preserve the peace. When at a disagreement, pause to pray together. Analyze the core root of the conflict - reaching a conclusion usually requires compromise. Don't assume to be right all the time. Avoid rash decisions and unintended comments. When things are getting heated, take a step back and cool off - people say things they don't mean when they're angry. Finally, for-give those who trespass against you. None of us are perfect - we can't be bitter towards someone for feeling flustered and frustrated when we ourselves are capable of the same thing.

Don't let the lack of communication break your relationship. If you can't have an honest, open dialogue without the judgment of your partner, something's wrong. Pay attention to your partner and try to meet halfway. Talk to one another. Inevitably, a couple is going to fight. I happen to believe that if a couple never fights they're either lying, suppressing their urge to, or is afraid to. Disagreements are going to happen - the trick is figuring out how to ensure that the disagreements are productive and even trans-formed into a moment of growth and love for the couple. Always remember, caring for someone means forgetting the self. It's preferable to break down and let go pride together and for someone rather than being right by yourself.

Prayer to Heal a Relationship

Lord,

In these difficult times, we raise our hearts up to praise You. May our struggles refine us, just as Your suffering on the cross revealed to the world the greatest level of love in existence: sacrifice. Help us to remember what is important and what good we may derive out of any difficult situation. Help us to trust in You and Your grand plan for us. In all things, Lord, help us to surrender to Your will as we lay down our arms and lift it all up to You. You know what is best for us, Oh Lord, and we pray diligently to beg for Your assistance. Using the words at the agony in the garden, we cry to let the cup of suffering pass us, but if it Your will, Oh Lord, let it be done. Let Your will be done.

We love You above all things.

Amen

Two Individuals Together

"Iron sharpens iron,
and one person sharpens the wits of another."
Proverbs 27:17

Ultimately, you and your partner are two separate people. While your relation-ship may have created a sense of "oneness", it's important to remember that together you form a whole of two parts. Strong individuals form strong couples. Therefore, whether together or apart, there is always room for individual growth that can later con-tribute to the whole of the relationship. Pray and discern together - the benefit of having a person to love and to be loved in return is the interaction and feedback that enables one another to develop. Challenge one another as individuals for the sake of growth.

Don't be controlling. Trust your partner to make smart, informed decisions and likewise, be honest and open with your partner in respect of their trust. Don't even be afraid to pursue common interests separately or different interests all together. In all things, work to always be rising in virtue and character.

Paul's Prayer for Spiritual Growth (Ephesians 3:14-21)

I bow my knees before the Father, from whom every family in heaven and on earth is named, that according to the riches of his glory he may grant you to be strengthened with might through his Spirit in the inner man, and that

34

Christ may dwell in your hearts through faith; that you, being rooted and grounded in love, may have power to comprehend with all the saints what is the breadth and length and height and depth, and to know the love of Christ which surpasses knowledge, that you may be filled with all the fulness of God. Now to him who by the power at work within us is able to do far more abundantly than all that we ask or think, to him be glory in the church and in Christ Jesus to all generations, for ever and ever.
Amen.

Progress as a Unit

"Beloved, I do not consider that I have made it my own; but this one thing I do: forget-ting what lies behind and straining forward to what lies ahead, I press on toward the goal for the prize of the heavenly call of God in Christ Jesus."
Philippians 3:13-14

"Then the Lord God said, "It is not good that the man should be alone; I will make him a helper as his partner."
Genesis 2:18

Make it a habit to discuss and figure out short-term and long-term goals with one another, the means of reaching those goals, and when appropriate, altering or terminating those goals. Focus on progress and define common purposes as a couple. By communicating well and aligning with one another, work as a unit to accomplish and experience things together. This helps to build connectivity and helps a couple relate to one another.

Paul's Prayers for Partners in Ministry (Philippians 1:3-11)

Every time I think of you, I give thanks to my God. Whenever I pray, I make my re-quests for all of you with joy, for you have been my partners in spreading the Good News about Christ from the time you first heard it until now. And I am certain that God, who began the good work within you, will continue his work until it is finally finished on the day when Christ Jesus returns.
So it is right that I should feel as I do about all of you, for you have a special place in my heart. You share with me the special favor of God, both in my imprisonment and in defending and confirming the truth of the Good

News. *God knows how much I love you and long for you with the tender compassion of Christ Jesus.*
I pray that your love will overflow more and more, and that you will keep on growing in knowledge and understanding. For I want you to understand what really matters, so that you may live pure and blameless lives until the day of Christ's return. May you always be filled with the fruit of your salvation-the righteous character produced in your life by Jesus Christ-for this will bring much glory and praise to God.

Handling Adversity

"Do not worry about anything, but in everything by prayer and supplication with thanksgiving let your requests be made known to God. And the peace of God, which surpasses all understanding, will guard your hearts and your minds in Christ Jesus."
Philippians 4:6-7

"And not only that, but we also boast in our sufferings, knowing that suffering produces endurance, and endurance produces character, and character produces hope, and hope does not disappoint us, because God's love has been poured into our hearts through the Holy Spirit that has been given to us."
Romans 5:3-5

It's a fact to say that there will be adversity in life. Disaster, personal tragedy, suffering - it's part of the grand human experience. In such times, turn to God. Hard times in life are inevitable and occur far more frequently than we would prefer. However, St. Paul gives comfort when he reminds us that God utilizes suffering not as torture, but opportunities for refinement of our character. Most importantly, the endurance of suffering and ability to overcome adversity builds resilience that strengthens us overall. The more resilient one is, the better she is able to recover from difficult situations.

When your partner is having a difficult time, console them. Try to share in the suffering of your partner by empathizing and understanding what he/she is going through. Most adversities require only time to heal. Be a shoulder of support for them in that time. Likewise, if you are suffering, don't be afraid to share how you feel with your partner. When all else fails, look to the cross. Christ suffered for all mankind, but for great reason.

Where suffering leaves wounds, we are called to fill with love from and for one another.

Prayer of a Confederate Soldier

I asked God for strength that I might achieve,
I was made weak that I might learn humbly to obey.
I asked for health that I might do great things.
I was given infirmity that I might do better things.
I asked for riches that I might be happy.
I was given poverty that I might be wise.
I asked for power that I might that I might have the praise of men.
I was given weakness that I might feel the need of God.
I asked for all things that I might enjoy life. I was given life that I might
enjoy all things.
I got nothing that I asked for—but everything that I had hoped for.
Almost despite myself, my unspoken prayers were answered.
I am, among all men, most richly blessed.

Boundless Kindness and Gratitude

"and be kind to one another, tenderhearted, forgiving one another,
as God in Christ has forgiven you."
Ephesians 4:32

"As God's chosen ones, holy and beloved, clothe yourselves with
compassion,
kindness, humility, meekness, and patience."
Colossians 3:12

"If you are kind, people may accuse you of selfish, ulterior motives; be
kind anyway.
If you are successful, you will win some false friends and true enemies;
succeed any-way.
If you are honest and frank, people may cheat you; be honest and frank
anyway.
If you find serenity and happiness, they may be jealous; be happy anyway.
The good you do today, people will often forget tomorrow; do good
anyway…
You see, in the final analysis, it is between you and God;
it was never between you and them anyway."

37

Give more kindness than you can spare, regardless of how you feel. Find joy in being generous and revel in the difficulty that comes from pursuing a life of good and holiness. Serve those less fortunate and those less able with no expectation of return and with all things, work with excellence and love.

Likewise, for the one you love, render allowance for flaws, forgive quickly, and give generously. Show your partner that you're thinking of them and that you care with little affirmations or even grand gestures. A relationship allows one to express appreciation without judgment. In return for your partner's generosity, respond with gratitude and appreciation. Acknowledge your partner's kindness and efforts of compassion. Above all, pay homage to God for the blessings in one another's lives.

Prayer for Kindness
Lord,
Help me to give more than I can spare, regardless of how I feel.
To those who live lives far less blessed than my own.
To those who live in great abundance to me.
To those who have just as much as I do.
Help me to give, regardless of anything.
Build in me a heart of unparalleled generosity, as You have.
After all, what I have belongs to You. I lift up all that I can offer to You
and my brothers and sisters.
I love You, Lord, and desperately want to be like You as You have
called me.
Amen

Guided by Wisdom and Prudence

"The wise are cautious and turn away from evil,
but the fool throws off restraint and is careless."
Proverbs 14:16

If any of you is lacking in wisdom, ask God, who gives to all generously
and ungrudgingly, and it will be given you. But ask in faith, never doubting,

for the one who doubts is like a wave of the sea, driven and tossed by the wind;
James 1:5-6

Make decisions with sober and rational minds. Control impulses and restrain the passions. When emotional, a person can make decisions that aren't entirely well-reasoned. The cornerstone of virtue is self-control. Therefore, practice having sound minds and encourage one another. Discern frequently and remain objective and open to many ideas. Be practical while at the same time, unwavering in the faith and Christian morals.

Solomon's Prayer for Wisdom (1 Kings 3:9)

Give your servant, Oh Lord, therefore an understanding mind to govern your people, able to discern between good and evil; for who can govern this your great people?

Enjoying the Little Things

"Every generous act of giving, with every perfect gift, is from above, coming down from the Father of lights, with whom there is no variation or shadow due to change."
James 1:17

The joy of the relationship is more than the big, romantic and adrenaline-filled moments. Throughout all of history, true love has been described as "gentle, quiet, slow, and, firm." Learn to enjoy the little details of being in a relationship - there's nothing like knowing your partner deeply and being able to meet them at where they prefer to be. Go out of your way show them you care, like tokens of affection via text message randomly in the day. When together, sit quietly and enjoy moments of just being with another person that appreciates your presence. Revel in the time spent with one another - life is unpredictable and you may not get another chance again.

Thanksgiving by Ralph Waldo Emerson

For each new morning with its light,
For rest and shelter of the night,
For health and food,
For love and friends,
For everything Thy goodness sends.

CHAPTER IX: PRACTICAL AND CREATIVE WAYS OF BONDING

So what can a couple do to maintain and even strengthen connectivity while distance stands between them? Plenty! In fact, there are more goals to meet and ways to meet them than time to do it!

Connecting Spiritually and
Growing in the Christian Faith Together

Prayer

How to do it?

Either on the phone or through video-chat, lift your minds up together to God.

Mixing it up:

-**Psalms and hymns.** Sing praises to God together - like a serenade!

-**Intercessions.** Pray for others.

-**Separate Individual's Prayer.** Find prayers you can both pray separately on your own time.

-**Common Prayer Time.** Set a time in your day or week. When that time comes, drop whatever you're doing at the moment and spend a minute or five in prayer. You can do this by yourself or you could call your partner - whatever works.

-**Writing Prayers.** Make up your own prayers together! Adore God in your own words and worship as a unit.

Bible Study

How to do it?

Phone, Social Networking, Instant Messaging, email, Video Chatting.

Set aside an hour or so as many times a week as you like. Bring your Bibles, non-bleed highlighters, post-it notes, and a journal, and go! Skim through it to get the big picture, take it line by line, reflect and of course, pray for understanding!

Mixing it up:

-**Cover to Cover.** There are reading plans found online that ensure you finish the Bible in a timely manner!

-**The Bible in History.** For every book you read in the Bible, look up the general time period it takes place in and the historical context of that time. With historical context, it really helps to understand the variation in cultural differences that are often attacked by critics. Personally, I think it's okay to go against the grain and stick with Wikipedia - it's a lot more reliable than people give it credit for.

-**The Bible Illustrated.** This may be a stretch from the previous suggestion. When studying the Bible, search for art depictions of a particular story. Art is particular to the artist's tastes, but it adds a bit of flavor and imagination to reading Scripture!

-**Different words, Same Word.** Sometimes a single word or verse can make a world of difference in meaning.

-**Formal Study.** You can find plenty online or in bookstores that ask questions and pose discussion topics that enrich the study experience.

-**The Movie Club.** Look up a list of films based on biblical stories. Read the appropriate story and watch the movie, keeping in mind the differences and deviations made by the film directors.

-The Memory Game. Memorization isn't everyone's strength, but it's always good to have some Scripture on hand in case you need it. Pick out a particular verse to memorize and meditate upon after each study session. You'd be surprised how fast you'll get the hang of memorizing verses, particularly long ones!

-**Guess Where?** Pick a random or favorite verse and read it to your partner. Have him/her try to guess what book it's from and perhaps even, what context or story the verse is from. This helps with the Memory Game, too! You'll find that some verses will be engrained in your memory - you'll come to know precisely where it is in the Bible the next time you need it.

Making it practical:

-For cell phone users who worry about running their minutes, consider doing the Bible study at night or on weekends.

-There are many free phone calling services that you can use through your computer. If you have an Internet connection, a microphone, and speakers, simply download or access the appropriate sites and call your partner! It's free! If you have a webcam, you can also video chat with your partner. It doesn't beat studying in person, but it sure beats just hearing their voice!

-E-mail takes longer, but it really allows two people on tight schedules to take the Bible study on their own time. There's also a greater time for reflection and furthermore, a written reflection is usually more rich in content. This also applies to traditional post - this method's more for the old-fashioned, patient-type.

Fellowship - Conversation

How to do it?

Talk to one another using any means you can! Phone, email, traditional post, video chatting. Sometimes, conversation can get routine or a couple might "run out of topics". However, there's plenty to share! A couple in tune with one another's activities and feelings build a sense of interrelatedness which is fundamental for connectivity. But if you're feeling a bit repetitious, mix it up! Celeste and I always had things to talk about, particularly with our conversation games and fun topics.

Mixing It Up:

-The Expectations Game. The Expectations Game is a question format often used in marriage therapy. Every question starts off the same: "What are you expectations for...?" In the blank, fill in an area of your relationship that you share together.

For example, ask one another "What are you expectations for... wedding planning? Vacation planning? Finance management? Physical affection? Raising kids?" The idea is to offer what you feel about a certain topic while listening to your partner's personal definition. By understanding what each individual expects, a couple won't be particularly surprised when expectations are or are not met. In fact, knowing such information actually dismantle a great deal of conflicts that might occur in the future! Even if you aren't ready to talk about weddings or kids, just speculate - it's still pretty fun!

-The Favorites Game. Think of your favorite flavor of ice cream. Then, have your partner try to guess. I'll let you decide what the reward or consequence is, but a couple can figure a great deal about each other. As our lives go on, our preferences change. Over the years, Celeste and I still play this game and we come to find new things fairly often!

-Phobias. As we get older, we come to realize the things that truly frighten us, whether it be monsters or loneliness. This conversation can be either light or serious.

-Short-Term and Long-Term Goals. Look ahead a week, month, year, or even 5 years with your partner. Setting goals help a couple to define a general direction for the relationship. The goals can be great or small and of any nature. Celeste and I of-ten plan goals based on what we wanted to accomplish, in what ways we wanted to improve, and what adventures we wanted to have within a certain time frame. Sometimes, we don't meet those goals, but we try. With these goals, sometimes we set a mantra for the time frame. Last year, we set our mantra to "Don't Quit" and stipulated that what-ever we took on, we would follow through to the end. It wasn't easy, but we did it and were better for it! When you accomplish your goals, reward yourselves! Celebrate all the victories of your lives.

-The Love-Hate Game. I love the feeling of the cold side of the pillow; I hate traffic jams. Figure out one thing you love and another you dislike. Take turns with your partner - it kills more time than you can imagine.

-Would You Rather Scenarios. Would you rather be fluent in all languages, or a master of all instruments? Would you rather have no one show up at your wedding, or your funeral? Would you rather watch a movie without audio and subtitles, or listen to a movie without picture? Would you rather be able to listen to any music in your mind or be able to watch your dreams on television? You get the idea.

-Mediocre Superpowers. Take an awesome super power. Then, make it mediocre. Flight, but you can only go straight up. Super strength, but you can't lift anything under 5 pounds. Complete telepathic control...of grass. Sometimes, you can go even further and try to find the best way to use your mediocre power to do good or evil.

-Thought-Provoking Questions. Once, Celeste bought me a book of thought-provoking questions. We've been through it several times, because there's usually more to discuss as we get older and more experienced in life. You can also search for lists of thought-provoking questions online - there's plenty to think about.

-The Rhyme Engine. This might be better done strictly through text messaging or email. Start with a word. Have your partner find rhymes to that word until someone is stumped and can't find a word themselves - that person is the loser of that round. You can also do that with entire messages. Try to line up the very last word to rhyme so the conversation sounds like a sort of lyric or poem.

-The Picture Update. Send each other a picture throughout the day of exactly what you're looking at with a little description. A shot of my toast and coffee before I head to work. A snap of a dog she sees out of her window as she commutes to work. There might be some apps currently out that do this same thing, but email or text/multimedia messaging does the trick, too.

-Or, take a day off. You don't have to talk every day. While sometimes, get-ting caught in the hustle and bustle of life may hinder you from doing so anyway, be okay with missing a day or two talking to one another. I don't want to say "communicate less", but there is such a thing as communicating excessively. Talking to one another is a blessing if time allows. A couple should make time for one another, but should also be sure to realize the importance of other priorities as well.

Fellowship - Activities While Apart

As this is a long-distance guide, it will be more about coping with the separation aspect. Here are some activities you can do even apart.

-Watching Movies/TV Shows. With television and film online through Netflix or other media outlets, you and your partner can easily watch movies or TV shows together!

-Playing Online Games. Celeste and I were addicted to Tetris online for quite awhile. With the technology now available, there's plenty of multiplayer game options that your partner and you can both enjoy on your computer or smartphone. Video games have quite a bit of variation nowadays - there's bound to be something you both can get into!

-Gifts. Sometimes, I send Celeste flowers for no reason other than the fact that I wanted her to know of my affections. Celeste would often bake me her scrumptious cookies and send them to my office. Send one another care packages, greeting or post-cards, handmade tokens of appreciation, or anything you can! I personally love a surprise present. A gesture or action can speak volumes.
You can also acquire coupons or tickets for activities. Sometimes, when Celeste has had a rough week, I search online for a spa coupon at a place nearby her to relax on the weekend. Be creative with your thoughtfulness!

-Visit when you can. When time and funds allow, drop by to see one another. The proximal connection is still important.

-Do your own thing! As mentioned earlier, your relationship is just a sum of you and your partner as individuals. You still each have your own lives to live! Pursue personal interests or activities, try new things, delve further into hobbies - the possibilities are endless!

CONCLUDING REMARKS

Let's recap.

A long-distance relationship may seem daunting, but in truth, it's really not that bad. While proximal connection lessens, there arises new opportunity for an increase in connecting on a deeper intellectual, emotional, and spiritual level. Furthermore, the time apart can also be an opportunity for individual growth, thereby contributing to overall couple enrichment. Take advantage of the time apart by discovering new ways to bond and turn potential loneliness into exercises for patience and prayer.

The real tricky part of it all is the impact the distance actually has on already existing relationship dynamic. People with good relationship habits will feel the sting of distance far less than those who don't. Therefore, the key would be to build habits that promote individual and couple growth. Focusing on Christ and following His teachings call for an individual to give generously, forgive frequently, and strive to be the best version of oneself are all key aspects of a growing and enriching relationship. Communicate with one another openly and honestly. Plan ahead and make a habit of working towards something together. The suggestions in this guide is by no means comprehensive - you might find other activities or even make up your own. The point is, of course, to strengthen your relationship.

Most of all, love one another deeply. Whether you're separated by miles or next-door neighbors, there is no substitute for genuine, patient, and generous love. If you're short an example, look towards Jesus, the One who gave His life for the sake of those who could care less for Him. Yet, we are forgiven for every wrong despite being undeserving. Likewise, love one another as Christ loves us.

Celeste and I will be praying for you and your partner. May God bless you and your lives until we meet with our Father in His Kingdom.

Made in the USA
Lexington, KY
29 July 2017